Jumping Thru Hoops

A Guide for Managing Your Criminal History
and Moving on with Life

John R. Lundborn

DEDICATION

This book is dedicated to my small, yet supportive family and to the handful of friends that have remained. Thank you.

To all those good people out there who help remove barriers instead of building them.

Good on you!

CONTENTS

1 How This Came To Be   1

2 A Double-Edged Sword   11

3 What Are Your Goals?   26

4 Knowledge is Power   37

5 Your Side of the Story   57

6 Housing   73

7 Jobs   86

8 Your Credit   94

   In Massachusetts   100

Miranda:

> O wonder!
> How many goodly creatures are there here!
> How beauteous mankind is! O brave new world
> That hath such people in't!

Prospero:

> 'Tis new to thee.

The Tempest Act 5, scene 1, 181–184

Visit the author's website at www.jrlundborn.com and

www.sentencemitigatorscom

Visit the author's blog at www.thedailycrust.com

Projects currently being worked on:

Nine Months on the Vineyard ©

ABOUT THE AUTHOR

John Lundborn has well over twenty-five years of police and public safety experience, retiring as a Chief of Police. He holds a bachelor's in law enforcement from Western New England University and a master's degree in public administration from Suffolk University. He is also a graduate of the FBI LEEDS training and a graduate of the New England Law Enforcement Executive Development Class at Babson College.

Since 1988, he had been a police officer various responsibilities and assignments. He was assigned as the police court liaison officer for several years, police accreditation manager and was the lead evidence officer for his department. He was trained and certified as a traffic crash reconstructionist by IPTM, testifying as in many complex cases. He was also certified in suicide prevention, crime scene reconstruction, crime scene photography and environmental crime investigations.

John has appeared, participated and testified in well over one thousand cases in Massachusetts. Upon being promoted to lieutenant and executive officer, he was in charge of departments operations and administration divisions, which included the 24/7 public safety telecommunications center. While he was Lieutenant, he had the privilege of obtaining full police accreditation status for his police department, making his agency the fourth department in the Commonwealth of Massachusetts to obtain such a distinction.

John has been an adjunct faculty at Western New England University, Bay State College and was a guest lecturer at Suffolk University. He taught classes at the

Plymouth Police Academy and helped implement his departments first ever citizens police academy.

John has appeared on regional and national TV, conducted radio interviews and handled public affairs for his department.

John has worked to help people with disabilities and those who are afflicted with addictions gain a more independent life through supports. He has done radio ads and participated in several fundraising events.

He currently is affiliated with a large non-profit organization specializing in mental health and substance abuse disorders and maintains a private practice as a certified forensic counselor specializing in pre-sentence investigation and mitigation.

HOW THIS CAME TO BE

1

There is way more "story" than I had hoped to ever tell anyone about my life. I guess that's what happens when you're someone like me, and you go through hell and back a few times. Of course, I saved that whole mess for another book that I started years before I even thought of this one.

I can tell you that one of the most painful experiences of my life is actually writing Nine Months on the Vineyard. Hashing up all of those feelings and documenting the incredible loss I endured is probably why I haven't finished it yet. It's painful.

In this book, I took my knowledge of the criminal justice system from when I was a cop and merged it with my experience of being on the other side of the system – the side I never thought I would really ever know.

Our society uses the past to predict the future. It also creates laws, policies, regulations, memos, guidelines and whatever else because something didn't go right before, or perhaps to prevent something from happening again. It is usually never proactive, but reactive, responding to someone else's fuck up.

Many moons ago when I was a cop, we had no coffee shop in my town. None! I know it sounds unthinkable. So we would slide out to the neighboring town and grab a coffee. Then one day, whoever was on duty didn't answer their radio right away or something like that, and well, that was it. No more coffee out of town.

Someone didn't fill the gas up after their shift was over – that resulted in a memo telling everyone we had to top it off no matter how full it was. You get the idea.

It's always because of someone who did or didn't do something against the grain or norms of someone else's expectations.

Our criminal justice system is largely made up on this premise. Reactionary, punitive and sometimes it's just plain unfair. It is also extremely political, which no matter how or which side you swing your hammer, is not all that great.

In 2014, CBS News stated in a report that more than 63 million Americans has a criminal record. That was then.

That is just shy of the population of France in 2018! Yet I am not surprised really.

This is unscientific, but I would bet that most of these people are normally good citizens that just got wrapped up in something stupid. I would be in many of these circumstances, booze or drugs were involved. Sure, there are those who belong locked up – they are out there. But I would have to say that more likely than not, many of these 64 million people might be a lot like me. Maybe like you.

If you are like me, then you know the meaning of working hard for success. You know about great losses both professionally and personally. You have had countless associates and friends become complete strangers. You know about the challenges and struggles it is every day just to start the day.

The National Council on Alcoholism and Addiction believes that there are almost 18 million alcoholics and addicts in the US. Again, I am not surprised. Drugs are sadly everywhere, and you can get booze easier today than ever.

How much you want to bet that most of these people are also counted in the 64 million with criminal records?

Remember the coffee story? Well, in that very same town, the only stores open were package stores. In Massachusetts, that's what we call liquor stores. Actually, we call them Packy's. Anyway, after 6PM, that was it.

I am a big believer that there are underlying issues to those who become alcoholic or addicted to drugs, or food, or tobacco, or candy, or really anything. I do buy into the addiction is a disease, as does the DSM-5. There is usually a malady or two - or three of some sort. Depression, PTSD, anxiety, nervousness, you name it.

On March 16, 2011, in the midst of my alcoholism, I can remember sitting inside my unmarked police cruiser in a secluded spot of the parking garage at Brigham and Women's hospital. It was hours before my son was to be born. After walking from a little local bar at Brigham Circle passing time while my wife slept, I sat inside that cold car, alone, with quick access to a fully loaded .40 caliber Glock. I can remember thinking how could I possibly take care of a kid when I can't even take care of myself.

I had a problem. A big one. One that I didn't want to leave to anyone else to handle or deal with.

I was close.

I sat there with my eyes closed. I could imagine the scene I was about to leave. And I sat - and I thought – and I cried for what seemed like an eternity.

I thought about a time back in 1987 where I saw a young mother absolutely lose her mind in the middle of busy Route 6 in Eastham, MA because her 6-year-old son just got struck and killed by a car. I can remember the exact spot, and I remember the despair on her face. I can vividly remember the pain she was feeling and how at just 19 years old, I was simply numb over the whole thing. At 44, I still wasn't ready for this responsibility. I could manage your crap, but I couldn't manage my own.

But what would that solve, I thought. I had a kid on the way that needed me. He would be here in hours, maybe minutes. How selfish of me. What if I had off'd myself. My kid would never know me and my family would have to remember his birthday as the day I exited – stage right. Somehow, someway, I was blessed by not having the guts to go through with it. Despite what the future would hold, good and bad, it was the only choice. While I hadn't even begun to deal with my demons, somehow I had the made it through one of the most terrifying experiences in my life. And despite the ordeal that was still too come, I got to do things most fathers can't do, like walk him to school every day and back and have "those" talks. What a blessing.

I only wish that I had that good fortune and inspiration on all my misdeeds, but I didn't, and I am not complaining.

I believe that people just don't get up out of bed one day and say "gee, I think I will become a drug addict." That certainly didn't happen to me, yet I became an alcoholic with all of the joys and expectations that come with it. And that my friends are what Nine Months on the Vineyard is all about.

If you bought this book thinking that it would be littered with stories of personal triumphs and failures, victories and defeat, sorry to disappoint. That is all in Nine Months on the Vineyard.

This book your reading is the result of the result of my alcoholism gone wild, and what can be done about it Yes, I wrote that twice. It is the result of the result.

My alcoholism spiraled out of control to cover and relieve the pains and maladies I was experiencing in my life. The result was my drinking and driving, drinking and well, everything. If booze wasn't involved, I thought it wasn't worth the effort. I definitely thought it wouldn't be fun.

The result of that was the outfall. Arrests, jail, a criminal history as well as a ton of other lovely barriers designed to make my life miserable – all in the guise of public safety.

My frustration with the broken system has caused this book, which is yet another result. Of course, some of this frustration lies within my own faults. I am not about to blame the system for my faults. I will take issue with elements in the system that prevent a person from the opportunity of positive.

I am a proponent of public safety. One thing I make sure of doing in this book is to explain why the criminal history system exists. I try to convince you that despite its impact on your or me, it is a necessary evil. It's therapeutic in some ways to bitch and moan about it, but it's even better to figure out how best to overcome the barriers of the system by using the smarts you already have.

When I landed at the boys' camp on the Vineyard for a short time, one thing most of the club members did was to blame the cops, the DA's office, the judges and their no-show public attorney's. I didn't. I blamed me. Of course, that didn't mean that I wasn't pissed off. It didn't mean I didn't have my own pity party. I did all of that. It just meant I knew where the accountability really belonged.

Where I live and work is a small place. You sneeze, and people know it. People are interconnected by blood, friendships or even hatred. It is a place that I still call home, yet today it is as foreign to me as India. It is small, peaceful, full of great people, yet vindictive, political and sometimes cruel in its own special way.

I had a history with many of the people and organizations that placed barriers on me. The DA's office, for example, my own police department, other police departments, probation departments. You know, the system.

The worst part is that like a coin toss, many treated me very different, very quickly – and that I hated the most. People can be so damn superficial. I know. I was one of them. It took a series of humbling experiences to change who I was to who I am today. I now pray for the bastards who condemn others. Perhaps we could all use a humbling experience from time to time.

We are not tried and judged by our intentions. The only real pain I ever caused through my drunkenness was to my own ego – probably a good thing. But in reality, the only difference between the guy sitting at the bar right now and me is that I got caught.

The big factor is what I did for a living. It wasn't who I was, it was what I did. If I worked as a builder, electrician or for the postal service, my crap would have never made national news. I would have probably been sent to rehab and returned to work hopefully for the better. That couldn't happen with me – and I knew it.

Before my eventual downfall, I never gave a thought or care about what happens to people in the system. I could care less about anyone who had records and barriers because of their criminal past. I didn't care because it honestly didn't affect me. I had no knowledge about what happens "after" – I was involved in the "before" and sometimes, the "during". Like everything, if people aren't touched by something, they are usually not passionate about it.

How many people are on the school committee without kids in the school system? See? Or better yet, how many were on the school committee when their kids were in the system only to quit when the kids grew out of it? You get the point.

People like me have similar stories, yet we are all very different and unique in so many ways. One thing that I have in common with 63 million other Americans is that I now have a criminal history report. In Massachusetts, we call it CORI, but because there are 49 other states and a host of other countries where this book will be available, I call it the generic term.

So what of all this? Well, it's simple really. I still face barriers in my everyday life. I still have to answer questions on forms differently than before. I have much more explaining to do now than ever. I guess it goes with the territory. I still don't Google my name.

This book for all intent and purposes is about management. How can you manage something that has become a constant in your life? How can you overcome these challenges and not fall victim to it? It may seem like common sense to many, but when doing my research, I can tell you that many didn't have a clue where to start. That's fine.

Remember, while not perfect, our criminal justice system is probably better than most in the world. The "not perfect" comes into play because its results rely in part on people's perceptions, public opinions, the media, and politics. Therefore, the system can become more of a sport; sometimes a game of chance.

Chew on these:

- Black and Hispanic people are disproportionately incarcerated more than white people.
- Men are convicted more than women.
- Defendants that use publicly appointed lawyers often have less of a chance of prevailing.
- The more "popular" you are as a defendant, the worse things will be for you in most court-related matters.
- The United States incarcerates more of its citizens than any other nation.
- You can get almost any job with any kind of criminal history unless otherwise prevented by law or policy.
- You are a product of your environment. If that changes, you change.
- Your past is ancient history. You are a different person today than yesterday.
- Attitude does make a difference, even if you have to fake it.

I didn't just dream these up. Some of these are based on statistical data readily available. The last few I have found are common sense.

I have brought these up because they all play a central role in developing our next chapter in life. Part of doing that is your need to manage your criminal history (your past) to gain traction into the future. Nobody will help you do this. You have to take the reins.

In the next chapters, I provide some suggestions of what to do and how to do it. Some work, others may not. It's really up to you and how you handle your own situation.

I have gone through much of what is printed here. What I have written can work if your at a situation where your ready to move forward. Forget the blame game. The cops don't wake up in the morning with the idea they are going to ruin your day. Alcoholics don't take another swig because their lives are terrific. Everyone has a job to do. So now its your job to get honest and get busy.

I wish you well and encourage you to let me know what works and what doesn't. You can visit my Website to contact me.

A DOUBLE-EDGED SWORD

2

The chapter title kind of describes some things in our life, doesn't it? It seems like everything I experience has an element of good and bad, for better or worse, risk vs. reward. In reality, this is how it is for those who are helping us to progress towards a better life and those of us who need that help.

For the purposes of the rest of the *Jumping Thru Hoops*, I will just assume that it is you who could use a little guidance in this area since it is you who is reading. It makes it easier for you to read and I don't have to spend hours going through correcting typos and being politically correct.

This book is about rebuilding your life, one step at a time by either removing or at least working within the hurdles and barriers that have been installed because of your past. You need and want a job, you need and want a place to live, and sometimes, you may need to start from scratch. Either way, you made a good decision by exploring your options.

No matter how minor or bad, your criminal history is part of your background, and it may (probably will) become a major barrier to your progress and ultimate success. I know, because it has been for me.

Let's face it, the last thing you need is one more thing that prevents you from moving forward – to progress in life. However, that is exactly what you have.

Society would like nothing more than for former offenders to get on with their lives and right their ways, but with major barriers installed, how can they? If I have said this over and over again, there is a good reason. It's a system that has not been thought out to the end.

Alas, the double-edged sword. I mean, you get sentenced for a crime, you do your time, or you get your sanctions and then your conditions. Perhaps you get out of jail or some halfway program. Perhaps you never went.

This is not like booze or drugs. You don't just go home and pick up where you left off. The criminal justice system doesn't care where you were in your life before going to jail. It doesn't care about what bills you have to pay nor does it care about your family life, your obligations, your job, etc.

Society doesn't really care either, yet their expectations are high. Get out and right your ways.

By the way, your credit now sucks, you have a criminal history which will preclude you from any decent job, you have a lapsed job history, and you're expected to show up to your probation departments door on a monthly basis or more with all smiles. Sure.

But what then is the alternative if you don't seek to better yourself? More crimes, more drugs, more booze? Back to jail? Who the hell wants that?

That's the unfinished part of the system. It lacks serious consideration to what happens after. And what happens after doesn't magically happen. It takes a lot of work. Those who undertake the work will suffer a good amount of failures in the process.

If our society is serious about crime prevention, addiction and the overall wellness of its Citizens, it will seriously look at changing the way we treat people who offend, particularly the ones who committed offenses fueled with booze or drugs.

We don't educate, we incarcerate. Human storage = time and money wasted.

Our system lacks the education and services needed to completely address the problem. While you're sitting in jail or sitting around the homeless shelter or at a halfway house, you could be learning how to make connections and deal with these problems before you get out, but that doesn't usually happen. Resources are limited.

Jails and prisons don't do an adequate job preparing someone for the transition. Many of them would rather paint the walls a new coat of fresh gray instead of providing an inmate with any service. I think there is a perception out there that someone in jail can get a Harvard education on the dole. Well, they can't.

There is one county sheriff in Massachusetts that wanted to charge five dollars a day per inmate to stay there as if the inmate had a choice. This same Sheriff is being sued because his facility greatly profits on the phone calls inmates make to families. The hits keep coming!

What about the psychological effects of jail? Most former inmates report and experience PTSD because of their incarceration experience. Any amount of time in jail can lead to PTSD, depression and certainly anxiety. If you already had some of that diagnosis it only gets worse. Of course, in most prison and jail systems, these conditions are not treated. Again, a mis-perception.

Shelters and other programs are obviously not jail and might have transitional programs. However, let's face facts; they are non-profits and probably struggling to make ends meet. Heavy caseloads and low client to staff ratios mean people fall through the cracks.

Our criminal history reporting system, the very system created for public safety, is often the major barrier to an ex-offenders future and is likely the major cause for recidivism. This is a product of our elected officials not thinking through the problem all the way. The result is a vicious cycle. Yes, I purposely repeated this because it is important and it's repairable.

There will always be the need for jails. Some people have done terrible things and are a danger to society. I get that. But jail is not the answer for many of the offenses that happen every day.

If society invests in education, it produces smart people. If society invests in jails, it produces ex-convicts.

Why do we have a criminal history system? The answer is simply public safety. Systems that report our criminal history and involvement serve to protect society. They are designed to inform and educate while attempting to not be subjective in nature, although that's exactly what they are.

All states have some form of criminal history reporting. The United States also has one. Our military has their own. Canada, Mexico and members countries of the EU also have a system. Interpol also manages a system. There are many others out there, but for our purposes, let's keep it local.

Try to understand the need. If you were searching for a home in a particular neighborhood, you would investigate the quality of schools, transportation, job availability, access to shopping and crimes in the area. According to the National Real Estate Association, quality of schools and crime are two major buyer factors in making home buying decisions. Makes sense right? Who wants to live in a high drug area? Nobody. Not even the drug dealers.

In another example, you are the father of a few kids and searching for a place to live. Not only do you want to make sure schools and crime are low, but you also investigate whether or not any level 3 sex offenders live nearby. This information is provided in the basic form to inform and educate that parent who potentially may move to that area.

Before I became a drunk driver, I came into a little bit of money when my father died. I decided that I would buy a few pieces of property in Florida so that I could build houses, retire in one and rent or sell the other.

After spending countless hours looking around, I found a few lots I liked in what looked like a nice area.

The first thing I did was to contact that Sheriff's department in that county to get an idea of what crime was like.

This was back in the very early 2000's when they didn't post those statistics online. So I had to resort to calling. Today, you can go to real estate Websites like Trulia and Zillow to get crime rates instantly. No phone calls needed.

The point is that the quality of the neighborhood was important to me then. I needed to feel safe, in other words, I needed the perception of feeling safe.

Think about what these criminal history systems do. In reality, they report data so that the reader of the report will make some perception of safety or the perception of not being safe around you.

I use the word perception because no reporting system in the world can make us safe. Just like no restraining order will ensure that someone stays away. Its perception in its truest form – a piece of paper!

This data is reported to allow for the creation of perceptions about an individual, by any individual. The person making this perception about you most likely doesn't know you or your story, or your circumstances. They make a judgment about whether an individual will be a good tenant, employee, volunteer or field trip leader. But again, remember, the data doesn't create the perception, the person reading the report does.

Imagine an individual that doesn't have a report. Does the reader automatically think this person has lived an unsullied life?

Later I will get into who sees what, when and why in criminal history reporting. I can only speak for Massachusetts, however many states have similar laws. I encourage you to go to your states public safety website for this information.

But that's why they exist – to protect the public in the name of public safety. That's one edge of the sword. The other is the one we are on. We, the ones who fall victim to the data and the perceptions from those who interpret it. Yes, I used the word victim because that's what we have become – at least in this sense.

We ex-offenders may have done our time, paid our fines, met our mandates and told to not do it again. We are then under the scrutiny of others who don't know us, never met us and who are deciding our progress based on our criminal history, or at least their perception of it.

Before I became a drunk driver, I knew about our criminal history laws. I knew how the system worked because of what I did for a living. I knew how it was used and how I depended on it to make judgments about people. Quite often, I would look at such a report and yes, judge a book by its cover. I would size the person up before I even met them. Unfair I admit, but that's what happens every day.

Just as we are all judged by what we do, we are also continuously judged by our criminal history for years to come. Get used to it.

You and a friend walk down the street together and pass someone you vaguely remember but recognize. You keep walking and say to your friend, "Hey, isn't that the guy who ran his car into the telephone pole on purpose a few years back?" It's not in our human nature to give equal weight. We don't usually say "hey, isn't that the guy who did CPR on that kid in the middle of town a few years ago?"

How the world perceives us is important. I know that like-minded friends have coached you and said don't worry about what "they" think. But you have to worry about what "they" think if "they" are depending on your criminal history to hire you.

You will see very shortly there are steps involved in the processes I have used and of course, like recovery steps, a little progress goes a long way. Time can be on our side even though we don't think so. Time - the only real constant that we have to deal with.

So, we know that criminal justice information systems are for public safety purposes. We also know that from that data, various people will render decisions impacting our lives. We also know that this will continue down the road for a significant period of time.

Here I have just listed several knowns. But what about what we don't know? What are those variables and how will they come into play?

Also, remember that we are the public too. These systems are to protect us.

The good news is that while these criminal justice reporting systems may appear to be cookie cutter in nature, that is, reporting data as only a computer can, people aren't. Not one of us is exactly the same. We have stories, experiences and can report bad things and well as great things. We can humanize data because we are human – reporting on our own human experience. The computer doesn't know us, but we do. So we use this to our advantage when the time comes – and that time will come, again, and again, and again.

Years ago, our criminal history didn't much matter regarding employment, housing or education. Unless you were going for a government position, the military or law enforcement, rarely would a criminal history be requested. In housing, it was almost never heard of. There were no mechanisms in place to even get that information.

In the good old days, a person searching for information had to call the police department, and have that police department call another, etc. Sometimes you needed to know someone to do this. Other times it just wasn't done.

Fast forward a ton of years as the information age took shape, and well, you know the rest of the story. Now at the touch of a few buttons and a click of the mouse, tons of information appears at the ready.

The world has become super sensitive to public safety. Terrorism, school shootings, egregious sex offenses, political misconduct and scandals and other major events have led to public outcries for reform. Now, we check everyone for everything. If we don't, we are subject to the serious scrutiny. Security measures are everywhere, checkpoints are the norm, and even the cops have bodycams now. This is the world we live in.

But are they unreasonable? Well, do you want your first-grade student taught by someone who has a record or past involvement in sexual misconduct? Do you want the airplane you are boarding to be as safe as possible? It's a trade-off, the same tradeoff we talked about earlier. What we gain in the perception of public safety we lose in certain liberties and freedoms.

But don't be misled. Having no criminal history doesn't preclude someone from doing the unthinkable.

Just because someone never did something before doesn't mean they won't. Just because someone did something before doesn't mean they will do it again.

A negative background check; one that is clear of any entries or wrongdoing whatsoever, will not ensure that the first-grade teacher won't become a sex offender or a child molester. There are also no guarantees about the safety of any airplane or the competency of a pilot. A series of protective measures installed in an airport won't prevent someone who really wants to create harm on a plane from doing so. Again, it's all perception.

The reason I reinforce this right up front and right now is that you need to start thinking regarding public safety instead of being the victim of data. I am not saying you have to like it or believe in it, but it is our reality. We need to develop ways to navigate through it instead of pretending it's not there, or worse, not dealing with it at all.

I know of a retired police chief (not me) who was on the no-fly list. His name was very common, and he had to get through this problem every time he traveled. He was frustrated and perplexed. He had never done anything to make it on such a list. Yet, even to this day, he is on it. And every time he flies, he needs to get supervisor approval with ID matches, etc. It's a real pain.

He does get pissed off because the problem is bureaucratic, but it's in the name of public safety. So, now that he is probably on this forever, he just manages the situation by knowing that he will have to show up much earlier, avoid the nice convenient self-check in methods and go through the routine. It's a form of acceptance. He is done trying to correct the layers of complexities in correcting this problem. It's frustrating. So he just roles with it.

Of course, the funny part of this is the story is that on several occasions, I was with him. It didn't help when I would jokingly tell the airline counter people that he might be a bad dude and it was smart to double check. Funny at the time but really not.

So, I have a criminal history. The first thing I had to do before creating a plan for dealing with it was to accept the fact that it exists. There is nothing I can do to change it. In time, if the conditions are right, I can petition to have it sealed. But in the meantime, it is there. I hate it. It is not flattering by any measure. Like everything bad that came with my drinking, I had to accept it and learn to deal with it. This includes the rejection, pain, and misery it brings with it. It's the gift that keeps on giving.

So, without getting too far ahead of myself, this acceptance comes down to having an understanding of why criminal justice reporting systems exist. If you can somehow come to terms with the notion that the system was designed to protect us from ourselves, you will be in a better frame of mind to design a plan of action to navigate yourself through this issue towards a better future for yourself.

Remember, you don't have to agree with it, and you don't have to like it, but it's our system as we know it today and you have to accept it.

Think about these simple concepts. See if you can just focus on these for a while. Try and minimize your biases.

- ✓ Master your willingness to accept and understand the reasons for the criminal justice reporting system.
- ✓ What if *you* were the reader of *your* criminal history report? Can you remove the biases? What is your first reaction?
- ✓ What if you were checking *your* report because your son or daughters safety was at stake? How

would you perceive your criminal history report? Can you remove the biases?

Like the steps in AA, NA or any other step based program, your journey to overcoming the barriers of your criminal history will take planning (steps) to achieve your goals. You will have setbacks and successes – and together we will go through them in this book.

A quick word about the Internet and Social Media. Yes, it's out there and it can be our friend. It will help us find resources and connect us to services. Life pretty much revolves around it. When it comes down to doing a quick background on you, the Internet is usually the first stop for everyone with some exceptions.

Simply Google your name, and you might appear.

Google. The Internet. Yes, they can be barriers too. Google my name, and a browser could crash. This is a fact that we can't remove, so we need to be vigilant about working with it. It won't go away.

Have you seen the ads on TV or on the Internet about removing all of the bad entries online about you? They don't work. Don't do it.

Most of the entries on the Internet will have been produced from court reports, blogs, and news outlets and of course, Facebook and Twitter. Police Websites often report their own news, and most police departments have Facebook and Twitter accounts. Then, there are the fan pages. Each time they update their site with new information on you, it generates more entries using tag words and entries.

If you have a name like mine, you will find me in a flash. However, Joe Smith will be very hard to find unless you specify some search parameters. There are so many times I wish I were Joe Smith!

When I was hiring someone, I would get applications and resumes emailed or sent to me. The first thing I would do is Google their name and perhaps add search parameters; like for example, Joe Smith, Boston MA., or Joe Smith Program Director. I would find something sure enough, even if it were something minor like Joe Smith was on the School Committee or Joe Smith responded to a blog. But it's that same search that can also lead you to other information, such as news clippings and police involvement, work involvement, political affiliation, etc.

Lots of stuff can come from doing a basic search, and there are no restrictions! Anyone can do them from anywhere at any time. They hit the Internet, and they are public domain unless otherwise protected by copyright. Even still, they are there.

I have said it already, but there is little you can do about things posted on the Internet. So navigating this is the best response you have, if you need to respond at all.

Understand this, there won't be an employer out there that actually tells you directly that they won't hire you because they Googled your name. But rest assured, they did. The response will be no response, so they won't expose themselves up to liability.

The same goes for potential landlords. If they Google your name and spend time finding out who you are, they will just tell you that they rented their place to someone else. They won't tell you the real reason.

Look, there is not a lot you can do about people who judge a book by its cover. They are at best shallow and perhaps self-absorbed. Maybe they're the type who get their jollies searching out the bad in people, perhaps to cover their own misdeeds. Perhaps they are blissfully unaware of their own shortcoming. Either way, you can't change that.

There is hope. Some people are out there that won't do this. It's like a fishing trip, sometimes you catch a cold, other times you catch Tuna!

WHAT ARE YOUR GOALS?

3

We all have goals. Perhaps you're incarcerated. Your primary goal is to probably get out. I know, I have been there. But what then?

Do your goals involve your criminal history? How do you even know if you don't establish what your goals are?

Just like knowing what's in your credit report before buying a car, knowing what's in your criminal history before applying for jobs and housing is crucial. More importantly, having a response to anything negative is the key to success.

You have no idea how many people I have spoken with that have been in similar situations as I have that have never seen their criminal history report. They make an assumption based upon what they think they know. This is the worst disservice you can do to yourself - denying yourself the power and knowledge of your own information – yet it happens.

If you are in jail or that kind of a setting, freedom and the simple luxuries of life are gone. The only thing you have is time – time to think about goals. This can be good, and they can be dangerous.

Even if you're not in jail, this goal building strategy is very useful in making a plan. And you need a plan to figure out what's next in life and whether a criminal background will impact you or not. Chance are it will.

I would caution you when thinking about your goals. Don't make them too lofty. That is, make them as short-term and specific as you can. Jail is no place for long-term planning. It also is not a think tank for success. It is not a hotbed of knowledge. Therefore, stick with short-term goals. As I will show you, short-term goals can simplify your life, add a dimension of planning and accountability to your strategy and are usually very attainable.

If you're not incarcerated, good for you! But short-term goals are still worth the effort because they will lead you to long-term planning.

Short-term goals are just that - short term. They can change, they can be achieved, and you can move on to longer-term goals. Baby steps are key.

A great method to look at a goal is to build it out as an outline. Remember, there really is no perfect way. These objective and action items can change, but they will give you an organized sense of what you need to do to accomplish your goal.

Also, some of your objectives and action items could become goals themselves. For instance, get a job could definitely become a goal. Getting your criminal history report could be a goal.

There are no limits to using this structure. I put it out there so that there is ease.

For example:

- Goal –
    - o Objective 1
        - ▪ Action Item
        - ▪ Action Item
        - ▪ Action Item
    - o Objective 2
        - ▪ Action Item
        - ▪ Action Item
        - ▪ Action Item
    - o Objective 3
        - ▪ Action Item
        - ▪ Action Item
        - ▪ Action Item

Goals identify priorities and specify how to intend to work toward something The Goal represents the guiding principle and provide a focus for more specific issues, recommendations, and actions addressed in Objectives and Action Items.

Each Goal has Objectives which specify the directions, methods, processes, or steps necessary to accomplish your goal. Objectives lead directly to specific Action Items.

Action Items are specific, well-defined activities or projects that work to reduce risk. That is, the Action Items represent the specific, implementable steps necessary to achieve your goals, and objectives.

Your goal can be as complex or as simple as needed. There is no limit to how many action items achieve each objective, especially if they are complex goals. The end result will look like a list of things to do, and that's what it will serve as.

Avoid far-fetched realities like *I want to be a millionaire*. Sure, we all would. But that's not based in reality. The objectives and action items needed to achieve the goals are not realistic either.

Example of an unrealistic goal:

- Goal - Become a millionaire by winning the lottery
    o Objective – buy the winning ticket
        ▪ Get a ride to the store
        ▪ Get money for a ticket
        ▪ Scratch ticket
    o Objective – collect winnings

- Get a ride to lotter commission
- Deposit money in the bank

Life just isn't that simple. Too bad right? But what are the realities in this? Virtually none.

Dreaming and having realistic goals are two different things. They are both good, but like everything, too much could lead to trouble. Keep your goals in check.

Here is a better example of an unrealistic goal:

- Goal – Own a house
  - o Objective – money
    - Action item – get down payment
    - Action item – steady income?
  - o Objective – make sure credit is good
    - Check credit score and details
  - o Objective – find a house that's perfect
    - Action item – make sure I can afford it long term

There is more logic to this. Why wouldn't you want your own home? But if you're in jail or in a compromising situation, you may be pretty far from that part of your life. You need a job, years of credit history, responsibility, etc. You need to look for the house. You need to maintain it. The list goes painfully on and on.

Also, if you're living day to day at a time and barely making ends meet, you might want to reconsider this, just for now.

I attended a recovery meeting once a few years ago. Some guy got up and spoke about his only goal to become sober. Of course, me being me, I balked at such a shallow notion.

"Why would anyone have a goal to become sober," I thought and then, unfortunately, said it out loud.

The debate started, but I backed it up. Sure, I want to be sober too, but it's not a life goal for me. It's a decent piece of a bigger goal. If all I wanted were to be sober as a major goal, life would be terribly boring.

I want to live a life that's full and fun. I want things, adventures and good times. Therefore, to achieve these lofty things that I didn't identify, I announced that sobriety should not be a goal, but an important piece of a larger goal. One that is far more fulfilling.

Of course, this is just my view, but I didn't get sober to be miserable, and it's not my life's mission either.

So, by stating you want to be a millionaire or that you want to buy a house is all well and good, but keep them real.

Let's stick to some short-term goals, like immediate housing, immediate income, immediate health insurance coverage, transportation issues, etc. Address the things you know you will need in the short term. Things that will take planning and work for a short period of time.

Let's assume you're in jail, and you are being released in two months' time. You need a plan and fast. Like many jails, you're probably not getting a ton of help but for the free advice of your fellow bunkmate. Let's also assume you have nowhere to go. You will be homeless when the doors open, and that can only lead to problems.

Sadly, this situation happens all the time.

Here is a short-term and realistic goal to obtaining housing.

- Goal – obtain housing
  - o Objective – look for program housing
    - ▪ Sober housing, ½, ¾
  - o Obtain a way to pay rent
    - • Get a job
    - ▪ Get references in order
    - ▪ Get applications
  - o Apartments
    - ▪ Look for a roommate
    - ▪ Obtain a way to pay rent
      - • Get a job
    - ▪ Get references in order
    - ▪ Background check?
    - ▪ Applications if needed
  - o Shelters
    - ▪ See if you qualify
    - ▪ Apply for admission
    - ▪ Is this feasible
    - ▪ Background check?

If you look at the goal, I broke it down into bite-size sections. Items you can take on one at a time.

Where you put your objectives and action items and how you list them is really not a huge concern, so long as they are listed somewhere as elements to your goal.

Goal building is a good activity towards building your plan. How will you even know if your criminal history will be an issue if you don't understand what the impacts might be? Better to know.

In the apartment and shelter objectives, both of those items might be impacted by a criminal history report.

Due to some research I was doing for book, I know of several homeless shelters that won't accept level 3 sex offenders, (the highest level) even though there are no families or kids in the shelter. I also know several shelters that won't accept people that have serious crimes in their background.

So much for the word shelter right? Still, those are the rules, and they make them.

I know of one homeless men's shelter that would not accept a man who had several disabilities, was using a wheelchair, a sex offender and had a service animal. The shelters response was they didn't have the staff to help him. Honestly, he didn't need much but a roof and heat. What they were really saying is that we know about you and we don't want your damn dog.

I told him to file a lawsuit and complain to the Massachusetts Commission Against Discrimination, but I don't think he did. What a good case that would have been.

The point is, the landlord, shelter operator or housing authority have established rules. They may all not hold legal muster either, but for right now, that is not the concern.

Think of a few goals you would like to achieve. Which ones might be impacted by your criminal history report? Which goals are short term vs long term?

On a piece of paper, jotted down a few and think hard about them. How will you achieve these? I will show you how to organize your thoughts so that they have some real meaning.

I have listed some basic examples.

Short Term (0-1 year)Impact Y or N
Sign up for SSI - Maybe
Get a place to stay or live - Maybe
Get a part time job - Maybe
Find recovery meetings - No
Obtain a driver's license - Maybe*

Moderate Term (2-4 years)
Get my own apartment -Yes
Get a full time job -Yes
Go back to school -Maybe

Long Term (4-over years)
Buy a home -No
Start a business -No
Get an occupational license -Yes

As you can tell, nothing is all-inclusive, and I don't know your particular situation. However, let's reflect a minute about the chart and then think about your own list.

In the short term, you may have just been released or about to be released. You need a place to stay. Let's face it, your family and friends are not going to want to do a criminal history check on you. But if you are applying to program houses, halfway and three quarter ways houses or even apartments, many will check. That's why *maybe* is indicated.

For example, in the short term box, I listed to get a driver's license. If your crime didn't involve a motor vehicle like mine did, then you can probably get a license without an issue. Generally, they won't look at your criminal history to do that.

When you make your list, really take a good look to make sure that your goals aren't too long term but ones you want now, or at least in the foreseeable future. I had that problem and had to really restrain myself from wanting the world in one week.

There are other ways to manage and list your goals, objectives and action items. If you're not so disciplined, just create a list of things you need to do in the short term. After you create the list, take each item and rank its importance.

I consider myself pretty tech savvy. I still get a cheap thrill when I go into my laptop and see the appointments I made with my iPhone, however I do this almost every day and still use pen and paper. This way, I can see what I need to do right in front of me. I can fold it up and take it with me, I can edit, jot down stuff, chuck it away, almost anything, using a simple piece of paper.

Grab a piece of paper and simply jot down the short term things you have to do. It's a shopping list, a daily chore list – only modified to reflect things that are to be done over a longer period of time than one day. Don't worry about following convention rules. Spelling doesn't count. It could be in the code for all anyone cares, so long as you understand it and it's workable.

To Do

1. Obtain criminal history background report
2. Find housing listings
    a. Internet, newspaper, friends
    b. Call housing resource center
    c. Can I sign up for unemployment?
3. Look at jobs listings
    a. Internet, newspaper, friends
    b. Sign up for help at the job resource center
4. Get transportation information
    a. Bus/train pass
5. Make a doctor's appointment
6. Make dentist appointment

KNOWLEDGE OF POWER

4

I know you have heard this before, but it's true. The key to success is to have the knowledge before you go and act. Have a plan.

We looked at building your goals and identifying if you need to worry about your criminal history. You likely do. I have answered this for you.

Stand ready for some hard facts.

It is imperative you obtain your criminal history report. Like your credit report, you need to know what is inside.

Look, I know it will be hard to read. Mine has a mere two entries, and I cringe when I even think about it.

Let's deal with denial. When I was active in my drinking and of course not thinking straight, I would go to get my mail like normal people do. After doing the street sort, you know, sifting through the junk at the post office, I would re-mail all of the stuff I thought was bad news or negative so I wouldn't have to deal with it. That included bills I didn't want to see, anything from the IRS, typically anything at all. Talk about denial! How stupid is that! Yet, I just didn't want to face the ugly truth about my life. I wasn't willing to be honest with myself.

You need to be honest with yourself. You probably have a criminal history, or you wouldn't be reading this book. You need to see what others can see so that you are well positioned to navigate.

You need GPS or a map to get around a place you have never been right? Same thing. So bite the bullet. I promise you that it will suck. I also promise you that if you don't know what is in your report, none of this navigation and moving on stuff will work. None.

Now, if you are still locked up, you can get a copy of your criminal history in the state or states where you have records. In most states, they are free if you write a letter to the board, committee or department that serves as your states criminal history database manager. You need to advise them that you are incarcerated and indigent. Obviously, your return address will be the first clue.

I have written a very basic letter for you. Feel free to copy it as a template.

If you're not incarcerated, you might be able to request this online. In many cases, you may have to use a computer to do this. Sometimes a small fee might be charged. It's worth it. In many cases, if you're indigent, they will be free but will require all kinds of documentation. Last I checked, many reports were ranging from $10.00 to the $70.00 range.

May 1, 2018
Executive Office of Public Safety
Commonwealth of Massachusetts
Department of Criminal Justice Information Services
200 Arlington Street, Suite 2200
Chelsea, MA 02150

Greetings:

I am respectfully requesting a copy of my official criminal history report. I am unfortunately incarcerated so I can not do this online or through any other means. I am also indignant and would request any fee be waived for this request Please send the report or any forms thereof to the following address.

I appreciate your help,

John Q Smith
Inmate W-29920
Black Bars Jail
2 Black Bars Road
Hicksville MA 00001

I know that at least in Massachusetts, they will respond to your letter by sending you two forms. The first is a personal request form and the second is the form declaring your indigency.

I have placed the Massachusetts Affidavit of Indigency and also the CORI Request form for your reading pleasure. They will look a bit different when they are mailed to you – but you will get the general idea of what they request for information.

In many states, the information your criminal history authority is virtually the same. Make sure you read the instructions to the letter. If you miss something, they will just return the form causing delays.

What you are requesting is the record that the public would get if they requested it. In other words, potential employers and landlords. This is the version they would see. If they see anything else besides the one provided from your states criminal records authority, it is likely illegal, or worse, a fraud offered by these fly by night internet background companies.

From my research, there are usually a lot of rules when it comes to your criminal history. How one would interpret those rules is for another debate, but generally issues such as who can request them, definitions and guidelines for use. They might come with your report or be available online.

If you are in jail and requesting your criminal history via a letter or a third party, such as someone at home or a counselor, make sure you ask for the guidelines and definitions too. You need to know what the language means in your report.

These reports are highly codified and rely on the heavy use of acronyms. Every state is different, so be sure to get the guide on understanding these terms from your state. It matters.

THE COMMONWEALTH OF MASSACHUSETTS
EXECUTIVE OFFICE OF PUBLIC SAFETY AND SECURITY
Department of Criminal Justice Information Services 200 Arlington Street, Suite 2200, Chelsea, MA 02150 TEL: 617-660-4640 | TTY: 617-660-4606 MASS.GOV/CJIS

Affidavit of Indigency (To Be Submitted with Personal Request Form
You or your client (if you are submitting a personal CORI request on behalf of a client), may be eligible for a waiver of CORI request fee. In order to apply, please complete this affidavit of indigency. Please note, you must select the option below that most closely describes you or your client's financial status. Requestor Details Please type or print clearly. Items marked with an asterisk (*) MUST be completed.
* First Name:

_____ Middle
Initial: _____ * Last Name: _____Suffix
Address:_____
_____ Apt. # or Suite: _____
*City_____ *State: _____ *Zip:
_____ Indigency Details *Pursuant to M.G.L. c. 6, §172A, I swear (or affirm) as follows: I AM INDIGENT in that: (select "yes" to at least one option) 1. Do you receive public assistance? ☐ Yes ☐ No If yes, select the programs you receive assistance from: ☐ Massachusetts Transitional Aid to Families with Dependent Children (TAFDC) ☐ Federal Supplement Security Income (SSI) ☐ Emergency Aid to Elderly, Disabled and Children (EAEDC) ☐ Medicaid (MassHealth) ☐ Massachusetts Veterans' Programs 2. Is your income 125% or less of the current poverty threshold published in the Federal Register by the U.S. Department of Health and Human Services? ☐ Yes ☐ No 3. Can you pay the CORI fee without depriving yourself or your dependents of the necessities of life? ☐ Yes ☐ No If yes, you must complete these boxes: Gross Monthly Income: _____ Gross Income for the Past Twelve Months: _____
If employed, please list your occupation and employer's name and address:
_____
_____
_____
If unemployed, please list your source of income:
_____
_____ Signature of Individual Making CORI Request
Date

Earlier I wrote that the criminal history report you are requesting is the one the typical employer or landlord will see. There is another version – actually several others you and they will not see. These are the ones generated for the use of police and the criminal justice system. This report is not for the public and in most cases, will contain every arrest, every court action, charge, probation violation, etc. no matter if you were found innocent or guilty. It will contain dates and the outcomes.

In Massachusetts, our consumer or public criminal history (CORI) is much different from that used by police or probation. That criminal history report is otherwise known as a BOP or Board of Probation Report.

I know that in Massachusetts, police and correctional facilities are not allowed to hand you your BOP, so don't ask. This might be the case in your state. They are not allowed to hand those to anyone besides other law enforcement, probation, and court officials. This is also probably true in a lot of other states.

The "public or consumer" CORI in Massachusetts likely won't contain charges and arrest that have resulted in actions other than guilty or something like a continued without a finding that turned into a guilty. Certain laws affect what is on there and what stays off or falls off. Furthermore, certain laws specify juvenile records, sealed and expunged records, etc. All of this information will be in the guidelines you request along with your report.

Your criminal history will probably contain probation violations if you have any. In most cases, it won't have a separate line item indicating that your terms of probation were violated and what happened next. In Massachusetts, it will, under the heading STATUS, indicate OPEN for an open case, CLOSED for a closed case, VIOLATION for a case in which your probation was violated.

The bad news – and it is very bad news: If your BOP becomes part of the court record, in other words, the docket or file on your case, the public, press or anyone can request a copy of that record. Yes, some information might be redacted, in other words, blacked out, but I can assure you that at least in Massachusetts, public records laws are nebulous and effect police departments, the public and courts very differently.

How do you think the press can comment on how many times a person has been charged or arrested? They didn't request a criminal history report on you, that's for sure.

Also, if someone were doing a background check on you and your criminal record did not reflect any charges, they could request records from a police departments report management database. Generally speaking, police reports are a public record unless they are open and actively being investigated.

So, if you were arrested in 2010 for shoplifting and the charge was dismissed, this might not be reflected in your (consumer) statewide criminal history database. However, the police department handling the matter likely has an arrest report that is subject to public records laws.

This is usually the case for every state. Reports with open investigations might be withheld to the press and the public, however, closed cases will likely be open to public domain via a request.

Let me clear this up a bit further. Let's say the police stop you for speeding down the highway. These days, they have onboard computers that will run your plate in seconds. After some interaction, they will obtain your license and go back to the police cruiser.

They can do a criminal history records check, driver's license check and an interstate criminal history check in a matter of seconds.

The information that police officer is viewing is not the same as what is contained in the criminal history report you will be requesting – the same one your potential employer or landlord will request. This is the case where I live, and hopefully, it is for you as well.

Once you get this report, study it. Don't throw it away, don't share it with anyone or talk about it outside your own circle of trust. It won't get you anywhere.

Read the codes, study the dates, look at the charges and the dispositions. Does everything look correct? Do you need further explanation? Is your name correct? Does your report reflect you or could it be someone else?

These questions may sound a tad over the top, but they are not. Databases are only as good as the people entering the information. There are and have been mistakes. They could have it all wrong. It is in your best interest to ensure that everything is correct.

Most state criminal history system authorities have a procedure where they can review your report against the facts of any particular case. If you need further information, they can usually provide that too.

It is vital that you review your report to ensure it is accurate. If not, you need to take immediate action, in writing.

Yes, I mention letters a lot. You need to do this in writing. Making phone calls is much quicker but less effective. Phone calls usually have no record. Letters are records, and you should keep a copy of everything, including the envelopes you receive.

Of course, for all of this, you could hire an attorney at $350.00 an hour. But if you're like me, you don't have that kind of loot.

No, your pro bono attorney won't do this work for you. They might return your call at some point and give you information about your case disposition, but generally, they won't handle this.

Now that you have reviewed your record; hopefully you have verified the information, and now you hold it in your hands. Now what?

There is good news. Time. Time is good news.

I mentioned early on that time was the one constant variable that we had to deal with. Well, each day, that report is one day older. Yes, I know, it sounds cliché. But, it's true. One day further from you and the offense. That's good news.

The other part of the good news is that if you can manage to stay out of trouble that report will get better, not worse. Yes, I said better.

In many states, some offenses on criminal history reports drop away after so many years, depending on the offense, severity, etc. Your offenses could be some of those. Even if they are not, if you stay straight, you won't be adding anything on to those reports, except time – and that's good.

Still, there is more good news. Many states allow an ex-offender to petition the criminal history authority to remove charges after so many years. This includes felonies.

To do this, you need to have no additional charges at the very least. That is common sense. You also need to show evidence of rehabilitation, and perhaps articulate job opportunities that could be impacted by the negative report.

I will show you how you can request a petition by letter. Many states have forms you need to fill out.

Like anything else, there are rules. Some states have a 5/10 year window on Misdemeanors/Felonies. This window usually starts when the charges have been closed.

If you are in jail now, you don't likely have charges that are closed. Therefore, this is not an option at this time. But that doesn't mean other things can't be done.

If you are out, never been in and trying to figure out your next move, you need to look at the guidelines provided in your report. If the rules of removing items from your criminal history report are not located in those documents, they will likely be found in your states laws, some codes or rules established by the state or maybe the courts.

Google - the search engine I hate to love, can help. If you simply type in remove criminal records in Rhode Island, something will likely come up with information on how to proceed. It might be the Website you're looking for or a clue to how to get it. Either way, this is a good start.

Be cautioned. There are so many scams out there that it's crazy. Make sure the information you're looking at is valid. Most state governments have .gov at the end of their website domain.

For example, a website like sealyourrecord.com is not your state's website. They are a business. I don't even know if they exist, I just used it in comparison. Get the right information or else you will be spinning in a sea of confusion.

I have included the Massachusetts request and the rules in the next few pages. I am sure your state has similar rules.

THE COMMONWEALTH OF MASSACHUSETTS EXECUTIVE OFFICE OF PUBLIC SAFETY AND SECURITY Department of Criminal Justice Information Services 200 Arlington Street, Suite 2200, Chelsea, MA 02150 TEL: 617-660-4640 | TTY: 617-660-4606 MASS.GOV/CJIS

Criminal Offender Record Information (CORI) Personal Request Form

If you have a valid Massachusetts I.D. or driver's license and are not submitting an indigency waiver, you may submit your CORI request online at Mass.gov/CJIS. This form is only to be used to request your own personal CORI information. In Massachusetts, it is illegal for an employer or any other entity to require someone to provide a copy of his/her personal CORI.

A money order or bank issued Cashier's or Treasurer's check in the amount of $25.00 made out to the Commonwealth of Massachusetts must be submitted with this form. Please note that these are the only acceptable forms of payment. Do not send cash, personal checks, or business checks. This form, along with payment or indigency waiver, must be mailed to the address above, Attn: CORI Unit. REQUEST INFORMATION * Are you submitting an indigency waiver? ☐ Yes ☐ No

Please note: You will need to submit an indigency waiver if you are indigent. The indigency waiver form can be found at http://www.mass.gov/eopss/docs/chsb/affidavit-of-indigency.pdf.

Requestor Details Please type or print clearly.

Items marked with an asterisk (*) MUST be completed.

* First Name: _____ Middle Initial: _____ Last Name _____Suffix (Jr., Sr., etc.): ____

* Date of Birth (MM/DD/YYYY): _____

Probation Central File (PCF) Number(s) (if known): _____

* Last SIX digits of your Social Security Number: ___ ___ -- ___ ___ ___ ___

☐ I do not have a Social Security Number

Father's First Name: _____ Father's Last Name: _
_____

Mother's First Name: _____ Mother's Last Name: _
_____

☐ Please check this box if you would ALSO like to request your personal CORI with your former last name(s):

Former Last Name 1: _____
Former Last Name 2: _____
Former Last Name 3: _____
Former Last Name 4: Apt. # or Suite: _____

If you are requesting your CORI for immigration purposes, and you have additional paperwork regarding the names requested, please attach a copy o

Mailing Address
* Street Address:_____
_____ Apt. # or Suite: _____
*City: _____ *State: _____ *Zip: _____
Personal Phone Number: _____
___Email Address:

Personal CORI Request Authorization
I hereby swear, under penalties of perjury, that the information I have provided
above is true to the best of my knowledge and belief.
Signature of Individual Authorizing
 CORI Request Date
                                   Authentication of Signature
Please note that ALL fields in this section must be completed by the Notary Publi
c.
This section does not need to be completed if you are currently incarcerated; ple
ase proceed to the next section.
On this _____ day of _____, 20____, before me, the undersigned Notar
y Public, personally appeared _____ (name of CORI reques
tor) and proved to me through satisfactory evidence of identification, which was
_____ (Ex:
Driver's license, passport, etc.), to be the person whose names signed on the pre
ceding or attached document, and acknowledged to me that (he)(she) signed it v
oluntarily for its stated purpose.

_____
Signature of Notary Public (Notary stamp or seal is also required)
Date my Commission expires

If you are currently incarcerated, a correctional facility official MUST co

mplete the following section.

Name and rank of Correctional Facility Official (Please print.)

Phone Number

Address of Correctional Facility

Signature of Correctional Facility Official Date

Terms and Conditions

By submitting a request for CORI using this form, the Requestor agrees to be bound by these terms and conditions and any and all other guidelines, disclaimers, rules, and privacy statements within this agreement collectively referred to as "Terms and Conditions." All Terms and Conditions contained herein apply only to obtaining information from the DCJIS.

1. As referenced in these terms and conditions, the terms below shall have the following meanings: a. CRA: Consumer Reporting Agency b. CRRB: The Criminal Record Review Board c. CORI: Criminal Offender Record Information d. DCJIS: The Massachusetts Department of Criminal Justice Information Services e. iCORI service: The Internet-based service used to request and obtain CORI and self-audits. f. Requestor: A registered user of the iCORI service and any additional authorized users for the requestor's account. The requestor, as used in these terms, also includes Consumer Reporting Agency requestors. The requestor, as used in these terms, also includes any individual who requests or obtains CORI or a self-audit report from DCJIS using a paper form.

2. Obtaining CORI from DCJIS by using this form is subject to Massachusetts General Law and to Federal law, including, but not limited to, M.G.L. c.6, §§ 167-178B (the CORI Law), M.G.L. c. 66, § 10 (the Public Records Law), M.G.L. c. 266, § 120F (Unauthorized use of a computer), and any current or future laws applicable to the use of computer systems or personal information. The penalties for violations of these laws include both civil and criminal penalties.

3. A requestor may only request the level of CORI access authorized by statute or the DCJIS for the type of request being submitted. A requestor who submits a CORI request using an access level higher than that authorized for the type of request being submitted will be in violation of the CORI law and DCJIS regulations and may be subject to both civil and criminal penalties.

4. An individual or entity who knowingly requests, obtains, or attempts to obtain CORI or a self-audit from the DCJIS under false pretenses, or who knowingly communicates, or attempts to communicate, CORI to any individual or entity except in accordance with the CORI law and DCJIS regulations, or who knowingly falsifies CORI or any records relating thereto, or who requests or requires a person to provide a copy of his or her CORI except as authorized pursuant to M.G.L. c. 6, § 172, shall, for each offense, be punished by imprisonment in a jail or house of correction for not more than one year or by a fine of not more than $5,000.00. In the case of an entity that is not a natural person, the amount of the fine may not be more than $50,000.00. In the case of such a violation involving juvenile delinquency records, an individual or entity shall, for each offense, be punished by imprisonment in a jail or house of correction for not more than one year or by a fine of not more than $7,500.00. In the case of an entity that is not a natural person, the amount of the fine may not be more than $75,000.00.

5. Neither the DCJIS nor the CRRB shall be liable in any civil or criminal action due to any CORI or self-audit report that is disseminated by the DCJIS or the CRRB, including any information that is false, inaccurate, or

incorrect, because it was erroneously entered by the court or the Office of the Commissioner of Probation.

6. CORI results are based on an exact match of the information provided by the requestor to information as it appears in the CORI database. Requestors are responsible for providing accurate information for the subject requested. In addition, it is the requestor's responsibility to compare the CORI or self-audit results received from the iCORI service to the subject's personal identifying information to ensure that the results match this information. The DCJIS is not liable for any errors or omissions in the CORI results based on a requestor's submission of inaccurate, incorrect, or incomplete subject information. Furthermore, NO REFUNDS of CORI fees will be provided because of data entry errors or other errors or omissions made by the requestor.

7. Each requestor who submits 5 or more background checks annually must have a written CORI policy. Each requestor is responsible for adopting its own CORI policy. The DCJIS publishes a model CORI policy on its website that may be adopted for use by requestors. If this requirement applies to a requestor, the requestor agrees that at the time of submission of any CORI request, it has adopted a CORI policy.

8. The requestor agrees that he/she has reviewed and understands all training materials regarding the CORI process and CORI requirements available from the DCJIS. Requestors are solely responsible for reviewing and understanding the training materials provided by the DCJIS.

9. Requestors who seek to receive the standard or required level of access to CORI for employment, housing, licensing, or volunteer purposes must ensure that the following are completed before submitting a CORI request:

a. Completion of a CORI Acknowledgement Form for each subject to be checked; b. Verification of the identity of the subject using an acceptable form of government issues identification; c. Obtaining the subject's signature on the CORI Acknowledgement Form; d. Signing and dating the CORI Acknowledgement Form certifying that the subject was properly identified, and e. Confirming that the requestor is in compliance with all applicable laws and regulations.

10. All requestors, including those that request CORI through a CRA, must comply with 803 C.M.R. 2.00 and, if applicable, 803 C.M.R. 5.00. In addition, CRAs are also responsible for ensuring compliance with the Fair Credit Reporting Act and with DCJIS regulation 803 CMR 11.00.

11. A requestor that uses CORI to commit a crime against, or to harass, another individual is subject to the criminal penalties outlined in M.G.L. c. 6, §178 ½, including imprisonment in a jail or house of correction for not more than one year and a fine of not more than $5,000.00. The DCJIS and the CRRB disclaim any liability for the improper use or dissemination of information obtained through the iCORI service.

12. Requestors are subject to audit at any time by the DCJIS and may be asked to produce documentation to

demonstrate compliance with these provisions and with DCJIS regulations (803 CMR 2.00-11.00 et seq.).

13. No information obtained from the iCORI service or from DCJIS personnel regarding the use of the iCORI service shall be construed as legal advice.

14. The DCJIS reserves the right to alter, amend, or discontinue any feature of the iCORI service or the conditions of its use at any time. Any such changes will be announced on the iCORI service and/or the DCJIS website in advance. The user is subject to the terms of use in effect at the time of his/her agreement. The DCJIS and the CRRB shall not be liable for any damages associated with the use of this site.

15. These Terms and Conditions are governed by and construed by, the laws of the Commonwealth of Massachusetts and the laws of the United States, without giving effect to any principles of conflicts of law. If any provision of these Terms and Conditions is determined to be unlawful, void, or for any reason is unenforceable, then that provision shall be considered void. The remaining provisions shall remain valid and enforceable.

16. By submitting a request for CORI to the DCJIS, I affirm that I have read and understood these Terms and Conditions. Further, I acknowledge, agree to, and am bound by, these Terms and Conditions, as well as by M.G.L. c. 6, §§ 167-178B, inclusive, and 803 CMR 2.00-11.00, inclusive.

If you think those rules were hard to follow, go and read the plethora of laws and rules about CORI. It's exhausting.

What's important is that you know your report, verify it and then hold on to it. Don't share it and don't provide it to anyone. This is for you and you alone.

So, what happens if there are errors in your report? Well, the first thing you need to do is contact the criminal history reporting authority and let them know, in writing. Sometimes there are instructions with the report or the application. Follow those to the letter. Address your concerns fully. Believe me, they will take the time to look over your concern.

YOUR SIDE OF THE STORY

5

We already came to terms about the fact you have a criminal history, you actually have a few versions of your report, you have people who wont help you through this and now you have some basic tools to work with.

First, you need to start making a list of great things about yourself. You will use this list many times, so don't throw it out. Instead, build upon it as if were (and is) a living document.

This list (let's call it the *I love Me List*) contains all of the excellent things that you have achieved over your life. Don't restrict anything. If you were a Boy Scout, say so.

If you helped Mr. Jones repair her house because she had no money, say so. If you are a sports nut, say so.

This will take time. There is a lot of good stuff. Don't shortchange yourself. List everything! If you think it shouldn't be on there, leave it on the list for now. This list will help you find ways to make yourself stand out against the negative that's already out there.

Just as it is human nature to remember that bad before the good about people, it is also human nature not to pat yourself on the back and take credit for the good you have achieved, unless you are a narcissist. Therefore, this is a hard activity and will take some soul searching.

Once you have a good list, think of the people reading this list. You have no idea who they are yet. You may never know them. But, you want to find ways to build commonality with these people, and this list is a great way to start.

Look, with all the negativity that surrounds people like us, why not take advantage of creating a list that positively highlights you.

Also, remember this. Early on, I wrote about how many people who will make decisions that impact us based upon our criminal history, or how they perceive it. Our criminal history does not help us move forward, so why not be ready to defend yourself with some really good responses and explanation that humanize our experiences.

Is shoplifting more acceptable to society if the suspect is below poverty levels and trying to find food for his family? Does a bad drug habit make stealing seem logical to feed an addiction? You have those answers already.

Neither crime is excusable, but in both cases, an ex-offender could easily humanize each scenario. And that's what we are going to do – humanize your experiences.

Start with a basic list. For example:

- I have
- I will
- I play the
- I am good at
- People know me as
- I am well referred by
- I was educated at
- My highest degree is
- I have lived
- I have worked
- I have been sober for ___ mo's/yr's
- I have helped
- I am a member of
- I volunteer at
- I go to church at
- I play this sport
- I can

Think about these for a while and add to it. Feel free to do whatever it takes to create the best *I Love Me List* you can. Look - nobody else will do this for you, so it might as well be you, and you might as well start now.

If you have been involved in the steps of recovery, look at this as an example somewhat similar to the 4th step. You are taking an inventory of yourself, except, in this case, you are looking for the all of the good. Then later, we tell whomever we need to get what we need.

Now that you have a good list, try and build a list of all the compromising or challenging things in your life. Yes, this will suck because not only do you have to rethink it, you have to write it down. This is not to say that you will need to use them, but it's good not only to be aware of these but stand ready to defend them in case they are called into question.

Not everything after *but* is bullshit. My father used to say that a lot, and I politely disagreed. I placed *but* after these statements because I wanted to show you ways in which you can control the issue and immediately expand to the positive.

Here are some examples:

- I was diagnosed with ____, but
- I need help with _____, but
- My family is _____, but
- I was abandoned at age ____, but
- I have been homeless for ____, but
- I have been incarcerated for ____, but
- I was on probation for ____, but
- I have been divorced for ____, but
- I have been unemployed for ____, but

Don't confuse this with aggravators. Aggravators we will cover shortly and involve things you have done personally to make your crime worse such as victim's age, weapons, etc. Being divorced, homeless or having a disability are not aggravators. This list, when blended with your attributes and successes will result in your final list.

We all have some good, and we all have some bad. We all have challenges and strengths. I ask you to find and list both. This won't be easy, which is why I ask you to do this now. Later, you will see how we can put them all together for our final product – our response to our past. This is how we can gain control!

I put two example lists together to create a final product. Look how I filled in the blanks.

- <u>I have</u> an associate's degree in business
- <u>I will</u> be graduating in May
- <u>I play</u> the drums
- <u>I am good at</u> golf and play every chance I can
- <u>People know me as</u> reliable and dependable
- <u>I am</u> well referred by my professors
- <u>I was</u> educated at UMass Boston
- <u>My</u> highest degree is a Ph.D.
- <u>I have</u> lived in Boston and Cape Cod for many years
- <u>I have</u> worked at ABC company for 20 years
- <u>I have</u> been sober for ___ mo's/yr's
- <u>I have</u> helped many people in recovery
- <u>I am</u> a member of the YMCA and the Lions Club
- <u>I</u> volunteer at XYZ skating rink
- <u>I</u> go to church at ABC Congregational
- <u>I</u> was diagnosed with Lyme Disease, <u>but</u> have made serious steps in my recovery
- <u>I</u> need help with public speaking, <u>but</u> I'm great at math
- <u>My</u> family is close, <u>but</u> we live all over the state

- <u>I</u> was abandoned at age 7, <u>but</u> since have been accepted by a great family and friends.
- <u>I</u> have been homeless for 1 year, <u>but</u> have made positive steps in my life by finding a place to live and a job.
- <u>I</u> have been incarcerated for 6 months, <u>but</u> since then have been a good productive member of my community.
- <u>I</u> was on probation for 6 months, <u>but</u> since then have been a good productive member of my community.
- <u>I</u> have been divorced for _____, <u>but</u>
- <u>I</u> have been unemployed for _____, <u>but</u>

You get the idea. Fill in the blanks from your list.

Once you're done, you have created a good working list to build a letter to a judge or your explanation of your record to employers or housing agencies.

The sucky thing about this is that you have to work at it. I mean, taking your own inventory is hard, but it's beneficial for you to take matters into your own hands.

Before we get into building your story, you should know that if you are currently in a situation where you can offer mitigating circumstances, you should do it. Maybe you have an open case. Maybe you have violated your probation, or you have some sort of hearing coming up. If so, these may be situations where you should retain the services of a certified and experience sentence mitigation specialist. That's one of the services I provide.

Sentence mitigation specialists handle much of the work related to crafting your personal mitigating factors and circumstances. Some can even help you build treatment plans and recommend alternatives to harsher sentencing. A good sentence mitigation specialist will meet with you several times, work closely with your attorney as part of your team, administer tests and testify in court about your mitigating factors or circumstances. Your lawyer should work out your strategy but don't expect him/her to go deep into the work of a sentence mitigator.

Anyway, if this is you and you decide to do it on your own, remember your *I Love Me List* will come into play and should involve some of the mitigating circumstances I described later.

The luxury about building your list *after* your case(s) have been dealt with is that you have the time and some latitude to explain your past and expand on the present. It will be all good stuff.

So what do mitigating circumstances mean? A circumstance that does not exonerate a person but which reduces the penalty associated with the offense.

In court speak, they are basic factors that lessen the severity or culpability of a criminal act, including, but not limited to, defendant's age, extreme mental or emotional disturbance at the time the crime was committed, disability, and lack of a prior criminal record.

Much of the entire purpose of this book is to use such mitigators to your advantage when it comes to explaining your side of the story. Perhaps they have already done this at court. Perhaps they never did but should have.

Mitigating factors are the opposite of aggregating factors. Some aggregating factors could mean severity of victim impact, the severity of damage, amount stolen in theft, weapons used, etc.

According to a leading legal consultant, the following list of mitigating circumstances are commonly used during a sentencing hearing. These same circumstances can be used to build your explanation of your criminal history report.

Here are some common mitigating circumstances. The list is far from exclusive.

Lessor/Minor role. The defendant played a relatively minor role in the crime. For example, suppose Joe received $10 for knowingly driving a codefendant to a location where he made a drug deal. At sentencing for his conviction for transporting drugs, Joe has a good argument that his minor role in the criminal activity is a mitigating circumstance.

Victim culpability. The victim willingly participated in the crime or initiated the events leading to it. If Domingo started a fight by attacking Walter and Walter responded with more force than was necessary to defend himself, this factor would come into play at Walt's assault-and-battery sentencing.

Unusual circumstance. The defendant committed the crime because of temporary emotional difficulty or significant provocation. This circumstance applies when a defendant acts out while under extreme stress. For example, suppose that Jesse, in anguish over the recent death of his girlfriend, stole some beer from a liquor store so he could get drunk. This point argues state of mind.

No harm. The defendant didn't hurt anyone and committed the crime in a manner unlikely to cause harm. The no-harm circumstance would be relevant if Harry carjacked a driver by ordering her out of her car, but carefully and gently helped her out of it.

No record. The defendant doesn't have a criminal record, or only has a relatively minor record.

Relative necessity. The defendant acted out of a desire to provide life necessities. This circumstance would be relevant for someone who stole food from the grocery store so that he could feed his starving family.

Remorse. The defendant accepted responsibility and showed remorse. A defendant who confesses upon arrest and is contrite in court has this factor in his favor.

Difficult personal history. The defendant's upbringing or family circumstances led to his criminal conduct. For example, a lawyer might try to persuade a sentencing judge that the client's violent acts are attributable to the abuse he suffered as a child.

Addiction. Drug or alcohol addiction contributed to—but wasn't just an incentive or excuse to commit—the crime. Addiction would be a mitigating factor for Joe's theft conviction if he had shown a concerted effort at rehabilitation, but relapsed into drug use and stole some copper wire while high.

These are just a few of many mitigators out there, and they are not one size fits all.

Now, can you see where some of your own story and your list works into the explanation? Again, if your legal proceedings have already been accomplished, then you have time to work on it which is great. You're not rushed, which is essential for a great final product. Time once again prevails as our friend. No attorneys are arguing and no judge peering down at you. Just you and your story.

Looking at the good side of bad takes some work. Let's take a situation where you are now dealing with a legal issue. Let's say you were drunk and in a car crash. Nobody got hurt, just a white picket fence got damaged, and possibly your ego.

So to continue, let's just say the evidence is overwhelming and you pled out to the charge. The fence was repaired. You even apologized to the owner of the fence, hopefully after you sobered up.

I can pull out a few factors right away.

- nobody got hurt
- the fence was immediately repaired
- you made an apology
- you admitted responsibility and,
- to date are living a productive, responsible life

You can easily humanize your own bad behavior. An apology is something people find hard to do. Taking responsibility is equally as challenging.

Add some of the elements from your *"I Love Me List"* with some of the mitigating circumstances listed previously, and you have a letter to the Judge.

In this situation, you may not have needed this letter unless the plea deal was not acceptable or perhaps the terms weren't great.

There might be even more factors. Perhaps you were out after work with some colleagues. Perhaps you were at a work-related meeting where it ended up with dinner and drinks. Think about it. Who hasn't had a situation where they drank a few at dinner and became a tad buzzed? Humanize the experience by detailing these factors in a way that you can relate to your audience.

If the circumstances were different, say you had an argument with your spouse or something like that, best to leave those details out. People (The judge) will start painting a negative picture right away. Of course, if that was the case, you should have a response ready for that.

Let's look at the same example but instead, this is your second drunk driving offense in four years, and you are trying to make a deal with the District Attorney to avoid a costly trial or possibly the risk of a bigger sentence. The District Attorney will likely play hardball, and you want the best deal possible. Always work with your attorney, but mitigators will no doubt be needed.

You will need to build your letter based upon your *"I Love Me List"* and the mitigating circumstances previously listed.

Let build the list again –

- Nobody got hurt
- The fence was immediately repaired
- You made an apology to the owner of the fence

- You had been attending recovery meetings for several years before moving here
- You were out with your boss and 20 other colleagues celebrating work related victories
- You're a great father, husband and sole supporter of your family
- You volunteer as your kid's coach
- You are often called upon, and people rely on you both professionally and personally
- Admitted responsibility (if your attorney makes a deal for you or advises you)

Ok, you see where this list is going? Again, many of the same elements are here, but I added a few because you are at the stage where you need it.

Are you a good father? Use it. Are you a good husband? Use it. Do you support your family? Use it. Has someone at work or at home asked you for a favor or help doing something? Use it. Have you ever participated in your kid's sports? Use it. Have you attended community meetings? Use it. It could go on and on – and if it does, good! Now is not the time to be modest about yourself. This is the time to spare no expense and really dig out all of your good. Remember, nobody except a trained and certified sentence mitigator will do this for you. Not even your lawyer is prepared to do this with you or for you.

Emphasize your dependability, your reliability, your value to your community. Make sure the reader knows what kind of person you are by you telling them, not by allowing them to make those judgements.

Are you a top performer at work? Use it. Do you have longevity at work? Use it. Do you have special skills or abilities? Pull out all the stops!

Remember this. You not the same person you were. None of us are. That was then, this is now. The old John is gone and the new one is here. If the old John were still around he wouldn't be writing this book.

All people change. Identify that you have changed!

May 1, 2018

The Hon. Joe Doolittle
Anytown District Court
123 Main St
Anytown, MA 12345

RE: Defendants Letter of Mitigating Circumstances
Comm v. Smith, Docket 2333CR-2022

Dear Judge Doolittle:

Please allow me to respectfully offer you the following mitigating circumstances and factors concerning this case.

I have been in recovery for several years, maintaining sobriety and helping others achieve sobriety. As a father of two, loving husband and caring member of my community, my sobriety is the foundation of my success.

As a longtime employee of ABC Company, I have been under a lot of stress with the lack of staff, cutbacks and more responsibilities. As a valued member of my company, I am always called upon to make sure everything goes right.

The accident of which I was involved is embarrassing to my family and me, and has created serious concerns within my workplace; yet for all of the bad I caused, some good has come from it. I have begun a long-term rehabilitation program and will transition to stabilized community programs when completed. My employer has granted leave and has helped me through this terrible circumstance, for which I am grateful. I am also humble and grateful that nobody was hurt and that the owner of the fence accepted my apology with good wishes.

I am the sole supporter of my family's economic stability as well as a valued member of my community, serving on several boards and committees. I am also the lead coach of the youth baseball team.

I hope that you will take these mitigating factors and circumstances into consideration in determining the outcome of my case. I offer them not as an excuse, as I take responsibility for my wrongdoing. I wanted you to know that I have the supports needed for continued success and the wherewithal for positive change.

Respectfully,

John Smith

Ok, some food for thought. The letter to the Judge, in this case, is assuming you pled to the charge. Remember, work with your attorney and never state anything that will hurt your situation. Also, remember that this is about you. When you in the middle of a shit storm, sometimes it's better to have someone else do this for you. Having a Sentence Mitigation Specialist can help you through this, so you have less of a load to carry. You have enough going on.

Also, the same holds true to matters concerning probation violations and probable cause hearings. All are good times to put your best foot forward.

Many of you will have already dealt with your legal conundrum a while ago. Therefore, you have the luxury and time to do this yourself. It will suck less because you're not in the middle of it, but perhaps your thinking why you didn't do this when you could have?

At this point, the past is the past. Now you can focus on crafting a good letter in response to your criminal history without the pressure.

Here is another idea: Take the "*I Love Me List*" that you made, and incorporate that with some of the previously mentioned mitigators. Then, next to the mitigators (good stuff), list some of the potential aggravators (the bad stuff). See where your circumstance needs more attention and focus.

Here are some examples of mitigators and aggravators.

- Good
    - In recovery
    - Long work history
    - Good father
    - Educated
    - Apologized
    - Sole supporter of family
    - No record
    - Church goer
    - Lived in town all my life
    - Volunteer
    - Time since last crime
- Bad
    - Long record of charges
    - Many years of criminal history
    - Used weapons in past crimes
    - Missed court appearances
    - Past gang member
    - Victim profile
    - Amount or value stolen
    - Recent criminal involvement
    - Caused injury
    - Recent drug use
    - Probation violations

HOUSING

6

Housing is one of those issues where your criminal background can really ruin your day if not planned out well in advance.

I have a pet peeve with landlords who improperly conduct criminal history background checks, credit checks, and sex offender checks. It happens all the time, and it's just plain wrong!

As with everything, it's all about perception. Therefore, it helps to make good out of bad if need be.

First off, understand that if your applying for housing that is owned, maintained or controlled by a public or quasi-public authority, (like a housing authority, HUD or something like that), they will likely conduct a criminal history background check on you. If you are applying for a federal or state program, like vouchers or any form of rental assistance, a check will also be completed.

Not only that, they will probably do a soft credit check and a sex offender's registry check.

In all cases, you will need to sign off allowing them to conduct the checks. They are not supposed to do them without your approval. Most often, they will require you to appear with a valid ID while you sign. This is the proper method of requesting this information.

In almost every circumstance, these housing and voucher programs will do this correctly. I mean, they do this all the time, so they likely get it right.

So after you authorize it, your criminal history report will be furnished to the requesting agency or authority.

The good news is that it's the consumer version (the report you have requested earlier) and the same one potential employers will get. In other words, it won't likely have everything in it.

There is more good news. Most agencies and authorities will work with you if you have a criminal history, bad credit and a lack of references. They are in the business of public housing and have seen thousands of people come through their doors with similar issues. You are really no different.

So, the best way to obtain housing is through honesty, organization, and by having a really good response ready to your past.

There are of course lots of exceptions. Sex offenders will have a hard time obtaining public housing. Period! If your criminal history mandates that you are assigned a sex offender level and must report your residence to authorities, they will no doubt want to know what happened. This may be the only chance to tell your side of the story.

This is one area that the criminal justice system didn't think through the entire problem.

Someone does what society considers unthinkable. He gets charged and does a bunch of jail time. Then fast forward, he gets out of jail. What then? He either is lucky enough to couch surf with family or ends up back in the system because there are no resources available to him. No housing, no jobs – nothing. Some homeless shelters might not even take him.

To say that's tough shit and he should have known better has been society's response – and I get it. It's fueled with anger and disgust. I am not throwing up some sort of defense of it, but that response – our response - is not solving the problem.

So, they end up back in the system, in jail or somewhere like that because they can't get housing, jobs, and resources. They probably do crimes to survive. Taxpayers will continue to foot the bill, at a premium no less. In fact, at more of a premium than it would be to get resources for this guy. Still, we complain and do nothing about it.

I know of a homeless guy who gets a mere $745.00 a month from Social Security Disability. He is a registered sex offender from a twenty-five-year-old offense out of state. He has life-threatening debilitation issues as well. He has been on every housing list from here to the end of the state - and beyond I am told. He has been disqualified for many public housing programs, and they won't even let him in the local shelter. What's this guy going to do?

I wouldn't be surprised if he resorts to selling fake drugs downtown or starts stealing candy bars. Back in the system, he goes, and we all carry the burden.

Look, not for nothing, but I have seen many people take plea agreements where they had to sign on as a sex offender instead of face jail time or probation. What a hook! I only wish they sought better counsel or found a sentence mitigation specialist because this impacts their life in so many negative ways.

Again, I am not making excuses for someone who is a chronic sex offender by any means, but I know in my state, someone could be urinating in public because they had to go, thinking nobody is watching and having no ulterior intentions, only to be arrested and overcharged by the district attorney's office for open and gross lewdness. Sadly, these cases exist.

But, if you are a level 3 sex offender, your sex offender report and your criminal history report will indicate this. This shoots up red flags for a public housing program or the agency. As such, public housing or programs may not be the option that works for you unless you can somehow get it sealed or expunged.

While we are on the subject, if you apply to a public program or housing authority and you have a criminal history report with arson, serious violent crimes, numerous felonies, weapons charges or drug distribution convictions, there will be red flags. These need to be explained away, or else you will not likely qualify.

Like I said earlier, many of these organizations will work with you especially if you're honest, upfront and nice about it. It also helps if the charges of serious concern happened a while ago, making time yet again our true ally.

If you had serious charges, say like seven years ago, and nothing else happened since you might be close to requesting those charges be removed from your criminal history background. Your success hinges on time and your ability to explain your situation. Have you had a more recent activity? Using the "that was then, this is now" strategy does work but only when your "then" is unblemished with more recent activities.

Be honest with applications. Many public housing organizations still rely on old-fashioned pen and paper applications. This is good news for those who are incarcerated since most any organization will gladly send you applications upon request.

The applications will likely ask you if you have been convicted of a felony and want details specific to those charges. Most ask for convictions, not arrests, not charges. Don't give them too much information. Answer the question and be specific. If you were never convicted, say so. Check no on the box and move on. If more information is needed, you will have your opportunity to explain that later in the process.

If you do have convictions, you need to indicate this and explain in detail. I would strongly advise typing your response on a different sheet of paper. Often, the application gives you little to no space to explain your circumstances. How the hell are you going to tell your side of the story in two lines?

I wrote a quick explanation of a felony conviction. I organized it so that the reader would quickly understand that I was addressing Section 4, Question 3. I also labeled this document Attachment 1 since I don't have any other attachments before this document for the file. If you did, just label it Attachment 2, 3, 24, etc.

The key is to be organized, brief and to the point. Type this so that it is nice and neat.

One other thing about public housing, vouchers, and programs. If they are on your immediate or short-term list, that's fine, but understand that it can take years for this to become a reality. There are two parts to this. The short-term part is the part you need to work on now. Apply for everything you can now. Get yourself on ever housing list, voucher program, and public housing program out there.

When I was doing advocacy work for people with disabilities, often common issue was affordable, available and accessible housing. Very little is available. I would always recommend that they apply for everything under the sun because they will be waiting a long time. I also advised that they need a short-term plan to get housing now, and not to count on those public programs coming through. This will be the same for you. Get on the list, but don't hold your breath. Believe me, the day will come when they send you a letter indicating your number is up. That is, of course, you update them when you move or change information. If you don't, you will become like the thousands of people out there that have been passed for programs because they didn't follow through. Don't be that person!

So, what about a private landlord or a real estate company? Well, this is where my pet peeve really comes into play.

Early on, I wrote about how the first stop is usually Google. We all do it, and private landlords are no exception. They skirt around laws by finding out tidbits of information. Let me take you through some scenarios and explain.

A private landlord who owns a three-story apartment house in Boston wants to rent his top floor. Instead of using an agent, he does this himself. This is common.

He might have posted his listing in the newspaper, Craigslist or Apartments.com. Either way, it's listed.

Let's just say the price is slightly below market which is still by no means is affordable – call it $1900.00 per month. He advertised that he would like security deposit equal to one month's rent, first and last month's rent and good credit with references. He does not indicate that he will do a criminal background in the advertisement but does indicate that he will charge a $25.00 nonrefundable fee for the credit report.

Fred is looking for an apartment and emails or calls the owner to arrange a showing. He likes it and wants to apply. So do the other 5 people who have seen the apartment.

Fred talked to the owner and applied. The landlord used the standard rental application for his state. (These are typically available online).

Fred went through the application and turned it in. He signed a rather nebulas consent form agreeing to background checks to include credit, references, and criminal history.

The first thing the landlord does is conduct a search on Fred, and the rest of the applicants via Google, Yahoo or Bing – whatever their pick. Using some very basic search parameters, he might obtain a serious amount of information about the applicants, or he may not. If he does, you know he will use this to disqualify each one by just telling him that apartment was rented to someone else.

Perhaps the landlord found out that someone similar to Fred, possibly even Fred, but maybe not, was convicted of selling cocaine a year ago in a neighboring town. The landlord, thinking that this is Fred, will simply bypass him for another renter. No other explanations needed. This my friends is not a proper check, but it happens.

Second, the landlord will run the credit checks on all of the applications at the same time. He probably uses a credit reporting service to do this since its costly do so on his own. The fee covers his costs.

The landlord gets the results on everyone's credit by doing a "soft credit check." This means that their credit report won't be adversely impacted by the credit check. It also means that the landlord probably just obtained credit scores and any public filings like collections, bankruptcies or charge-offs. In other words, very basic information just to qualify.

Then, the landlord would check references. In Fred's case, let's say his references are ok and verifiable.

For the purposes of this example, let's say the landlord found out that Fred called the police a lot on his neighbors a few years ago. Like before, the landlord will simply skip Fred and just tell him that the apartment was leased to someone else, no chance for explanations.

I have a problem with a few issues here.

1. If a potential landlord is going to rely on your credit to help him make a leasing decision, then that landlord should report your payments like credit card companies do. If he did, your on-time payments for housing, which is significantly large, would reflect very favorably on your credit report. But there is no requirement to do this. So much for continuity and helping renters out!

2. Also, yet again, another decision is made with the help of Google, Yahoo or Bing! The landlord, having searched out Fred on the internet, found information. How can he verify this? How can he make a decision based solely on web searches?

Can he make a decision not to lease to him based on Fred's reputation and character posted online? Not really. What he would do is just respond with "I rented it to someone else."

This happens with private landlords. I have heard horror stories and spoken to countless people who were on the other side of this. Don't be surprised or shocked that you didn't get to lease the apartment you liked because "somebody beat you to it." Sure, this could be legit, but many times it's just the excuse they use to not rent to you.

Larger companies that own portfolios of apartments will not likely use this method. First, they have a lot of apartments to rent, and turnover costs money. Second, they use standardized forms and have contacts with other companies that do backgrounds and credit. They are also upfront with letting you know that they check criminal history, sex offender, and credit. They often have qualifiers such as no pets, income at a certain level or higher and one car max.

In the case of a large management company running or owning an apartment you want to rent, many times the application is online. They will ask you about your background as allowed by law in your state. Be honest. Just like in the scenario involving public housing, its best, to be honest, concise and to the point if it comes down to explaining your situation. The good news is that barring any very serious and recent crimes, many of these places will rent to you. Of course, you will be paying a premium as these places are never cheap. They are more interested in filling the apartment and ensuring their bottom line is profitable than your background. They care more about your ability to pay than anything.

Of course, the landlord that owns the three family apartment is also concerned about the bottom line, but he may be an active member of his community. If he is a local landlord, then chances are he lives, works and raised a family close by. Therefore, he has much more stake in his community than the big management companies.

See the differences? It just depends on who you're doing business with. It also depends on your ability to write a good response to your criminal history should you have too.

Many times, that same community-minded local landlord might have a brother or friend that was jammed up and ran into problems along the way. Maybe they are willing to rent to you because they want to give you a chance or think you are a nice person. Sometimes, that's all you need. Something that links you to them and humanizes your issues.

Of course, there are always landlords out there who don't check anything. Sometimes, they will be renting out the basement of their mother in laws house. I cast no judgments. Just beware and do your due diligence. Maybe this is ok for right now. It's easier to find an apartment when you're living in an apartment. It's also easier finding a job when you have a job.

Attachment 1

John Q Citizen
Answer to Section 4, Question 3
Have you ever been convicted of a felony?

On June 20, 2010 I was arrested and subsequently convicted of larceny of a motor vehicle via a plea agreement with the Suffolk County District Attorney's Office.

The entire event was a big misunderstanding. I borrowed a car from a friend to go on a job interview. I was stopped for speeding. A police check revealed that the vehicle was reported stolen. I had no idea the vehicle was stolen as I believed it had belonged to my friend. I had no knowledge of this and have found the entire situation rather embarrassing. In hind sight, I should have seen that the car was registered in New Jersey but at the time, I thought nothing of it.

I could not afford an attorney at the time and agreed to the above referenced disposition to just move on from the incident.

Since that time, I have been in no trouble. I have graduated college and maintained a high GPA. I have been working at ABC company for several years and consider myself to be a good citizen.

Also, I plan on petitioning the Board of Probation to seek removal of this entry when the law allows.

Thank you for your consideration.

May 1, 2018

Mrs. McGee
Mayfield Housing Authority
123 Smith Drive
Anytown, MA 02122

RE:Explanation of Criminal History Report

Dear Ms. McGee:

Thank you for contacting me regarding my criminal history background and for allowing me the opportunity to respond and comment.

I was abused as a child and was sent out to 6 different foster homes. I never had a real family and never learned right from wrong. The only cure for my emptiness was to associate with people who would make me feel I belonged. I knew they were bad, but the accepted me more than anyone. Then I got into drugs, and my world became a nightmare.

One or two short paragraphs and already the reader understands that your life has seen its share of troubles. People can and will relate if you make it easy for them. Don't make them dig, tell them all about it by being short, sweet, to the point and without blaming someone. Show that you are thankful, grateful and filled with gratitude.

Finally, after being on the street, using every drug out there and doing everything to support my habit, I was arrested trying to steal from a local store. I am actually grateful that this happened because this was the end. I knew that my life would change for the better. Someone had to stop the cycle, and I knew it wasn't me.

Since that dark time, I have been a loving father to my two sons. People know me and trust me, and I come well referred professionally and personally. I have been sober for over one year, work a vigorous program, and have faith and now investigating new exciting educational opportunities. I volunteer at my local homeless shelter one day a week, go to church and have become a good citizen of my community.

I hope you can understand what I went through as a younger man. I am a changed person and grateful for the chance to change. I appreciate the opportunity to explain this difficult situation and remain hopeful of being selected for a unit at Mayfield Housing Authority.

Sincerely,
Joe Smith
Housing Applicant

JOBS

7

Many jobs out there don't do much in the way of checking you out. If you're planning to join up with a landscaping crew or banging some nails, it is highly unlikely that a criminal background check will be done.

A lot of big box retailers don't do criminal history backgrounds either unless the employee is a key holder or handles the cash. So, if you are looking to get working rather quickly, you might want to try your local mall. That's not to say that all of these establishments are the same. I happen to know that McDonald's, Burger King and Wendy's all do criminal history background checks. Generally speaking, a good rule of thumb to use when applying to jobs is to go in with the understanding that the potential employer will do a check on you.

As a matter of public policy, local, state and federal governments will always conduct a criminal history background check, a driving history and in some cases a soft credit check. You can count on it.

But, having a criminal background should not deter you from going after the job you want. If you're qualified, have a resume to back your skills and abilities up, go for it. Your criminal background can be explained.

There are many ways that potential employers can find out information. There are many databases out there containing your information.

Let's look at this very common scenario: Fred had been arrested in Boston, MA for shoplifting in 2012. The charge was continued without a finding for one year. He paid a fine. No probation or anything else. The charge was a misdemeanor, and the item he stole was a candy bar.

Ok, if he never got another charge after this, the CORI would likely reflect "no record" and wouldn't have the charge on it. It would be clean.

However, let's say Fred is applying for a job with the state. They would as a matter of policy conduct a CORI. The CORI would probably come back with nothing on it. However, in their background investigation, let's assume they pulled police reports matching Fred's address for the last seven years. They would possibly reveal that Fred was indeed arrested by Boston PD. The records in his case through the police department would be public except where the law mandates redaction. Also, since Fred was arrested and there was court action, any record at the court would be public as well, save the parts they would have to react.

So having a clean CORI is great, but some records will be revealed during a background investigation. As such, you will need to explain this to the hiring authority when it's time to respond to their investigation.

Ok, Fred's example is common if he were applying for a municipal, state or federal job, but maybe not in your case. Many employers will rely on the CORI alone.

Let's look at this case. Let's assume Sally got arrested by state police for OUI (first offense) back in 2017. Since then, Sally has had no criminal history. Sally, through a plea bargain, received a continued without a finding (CWOF) for a year, fines and a first offenders program. She completed everything and has maintained an unsullied life.

Sally applied to a large, local nonprofit working with kids in the Boston area. Part of the job required her to drive a van from time to time.

She gets hired, and the organization as a matter of policy conducts a CORI. Nothing comes back on her CORI. They pull a driving record and discover the OUI through that report. They then retrieve the public record through the state police. She will need to explain the situation fully.

All too many times, mental health, personal tragedy, family history and abuse comes into play in a lot of these circumstances. If that's the case, you need to figure out if you're ready to go there or not.

He is a sample statement from someone who would have a few drug convictions and related crimes on their criminal history report."

"I was abused as a child and was sent out to 6 different foster homes. I never had a real family and never learned right from wrong. The only cure for my emptiness was to associate with people who would make me feel I belonged. I knew they were bad, but the accepted me more than anyone. Then I got into drugs, and my world became a nightmare."

In this example, five sentences and already the reader understands that your life has seen its share of troubles. Many people can and will relate if you make it easy for them. Don't make them dig, tell them all about it by being short, sweet, to the point and without blaming someone. Show that you are thankful, grateful and filled with gratitude.

"Finally, after being on the street for a what seemed like an eternity, using every drug out there and doing everything to support my habit, I was arrested trying to steal from a local store. I am actually grateful that this happened because this was the end. I knew that my life would have to change for the better because it couldn't get any worse. Someone had to stop the cycle, and I knew it wasn't me."

Remember that list? -

"Since that dark time, I have been a loving father to my two sons. People know me and trust me, and I come well referred professionally and personally. I have been sober for over one year,

work a vigorous program, and have a renewed sense of faith and now investigating new exciting educational opportunities. I volunteer at my local homeless shelter one day a week, go to church and have become a good citizen. This may sound strange, but I am thankful I was arrested because my cycle of addiction stopped."

Let's take a look at this response all assembled and put together. In this example remember, we are responding to some drug convictions and maybe larceny or theft convictions. We are positive. We are not making excuses, just offering some reasons why things turned out the way they did.

May 1, 2018

Mrs. McGee
Human Resources
ABC Company
100 Commonwealth Ave
Boston MA 02111

RE: Explanation of Criminal History Report

Dear Ms. McGee:

Thank you for contacting me regarding my criminal history background and for allowing me the opportunity to respond and comment.

I was abused and neglected as a child, which resulted in being sent out to 6 different foster homes. I never had a real family and never learned right from wrong. The only cure for my emptiness was to associate with people (anybody) who would make me feel I belonged. I knew they were bad, but they accepted me more than anyone. Then I got into drugs, and my world became a nightmare.

Finally, after being on the street for several years, using every drug and doing everything to support my habit, I was arrested trying to steal from a local store. I am actually grateful that this happened because this was the end. I knew that my life would change for the better. Someone had to stop the cycle, and I knew it wasn't me.

Since that dark time, I have been a loving father to my two sons. People know me and trust me, and I come well referred professionally and personally. I have been sober for over one year, work a vigorous program, and have faith and now investigating new exciting educational opportunities. I volunteer at my local homeless shelter one day a week, go to church and have become a good citizen of my community.

I hope you can understand what I went through as a younger man. I am a changed person and grateful for the chance to change. I appreciate the opportunity to explain this difficult situation. I remain eager to work with ABC Company.

Sincerely,
Joe Smith
Applicant for the Position of Engineer

Of course, this is one example of many we could come up with, but do you see the point? Short, simple and polite. Well formatted and professional. That's the objective.

An important piece in crafting your story is by being empathic to your reader at the same time, humanizing your story.

Let's say for example that ABC Co. wanted to hire you and asked you to submit to a criminal history background check. You did, and it came back with issues. As such, ABC has requested an explanation from you for the history on the report.

You wrote the letter above in response. Good. But if you know or get the feeling you might not get the job because of the report, you may want to emphasize or change the last paragraph.

For example, writing something like

> "While I would consider it extremely unfortunate, I would very much understand if I am no longer qualified as a candidate for ABC Company because of my past. I understand the needs for adhering to company policy. Please allow me to reiterate that my past is not reflective of who I am today. But for this barrier, I know I would be a rising star at ABC. Perhaps, in light of my circumstance backed with my qualifications and experience, ABC could see its way to continuing my candidacy for the position. I can guarantee that giving me a chance will be a great decision ABC could make without regret."

Again, this is just an example, but it's an important one. It is well written, empathetic to the needs of employers, understanding of the employer's policies and reflects your desire to be an employee. It also humanizes your criminal history report regardless of what it said.

YOUR CREDIT

8

Since we are on the topic or reports that impact your life, I figured I would mention a few words about credit. I know it sucks, but credit reports are a fact of life and a popular measurement for jobs, housing, and business opportunities.

If you have been incarcerated, you might be one of few lucky ones that have someone on the outside that is looking after your matters. Such a rarity.

A good bankruptcy attorney once told me that people who are incarcerated for over 4 months that have nobody helping them and have considerable debt should just file for bankruptcy when they get out. It kind of makes sense really. How are you going to enter into agreements and pay back old credit card bills while your credit rating is below 540 and your job pays hardly anything?

You don't have to be incarcerated to relate to all of this as it might apply.

Credit reports have a lot in common with criminal history background reports. Just like your criminal history, your credit report can be explained as well.

There are more similarities, Time. That's right. Time. Time can help your credit report – or hurt it.

So, let's say you don't have any outstanding debt to speak of and you have credit cards. Your one of the lucky ones. There is no sense in filing since you have nothing to claim as debt. But you will need to get your credit score up there. Time will help and opening a new card account will help too.

If you are in too deep, you might want to consider filing. Another painful chapter in your life but one that will bring closure on a lot of old debt while wiping your slate clean for the future.

My understanding is that the only things you really can't wipe out from a chapter 7 bankruptcy filing are student loan department, taxes, child support and court fines. Also, previous judgments from old lawsuits may not be erased either. Any good bankruptcy attorney will give you the low down. Most will give you a consultation for free. Last time I checked, depending on your situation, fees for filing ranged from $1800 to $3500. Of course, if you own a house or three, a business and have money in the bank, things change. But a simple bankruptcy filing for someone having no property, assets or money in the bank can do this relatively cheap.

It takes a while too. There is a boatload of paperwork, fact-finding, and document researching on your part. Generally, it can take a year to go through the motions to get your case discharged by a judge. Then, the nasty bankruptcy statement gets entered on your credit report. This will be there anywhere from 3 years to 10 years, depending on where you live and the type of filing you did.

But, the great news is that with the discharge, all of your old debts were wiped away, and you owe nothing. Freedom? Sort of.

That negative entry will be a barrier, but like all things, time will heal this too.

Here are a few pointers. I know. I have used some of these strategies to build credit.

The key to good credit is having a steady stream of income. You need not be a millionaire, but you need a reliable, dependable, steady stream. Again, time on your job could be a factor. If you're disabled, your SSI could be that steady stream.

The other key is paying on time, every time.

Many lenders out there overlook bankruptcy filings. In fact, some disregard them totally and sustain the risk of lending you money for a higher interest rate.

So, let's say you filed chapter 7, and it got discharged. What then.

If I were you, I would go and apply for a credit card. Yes, you read that right. Open one of those easy to get, low credit limit high-interest credit cards. Sometimes, it might be one of those secure cards. Who cares? The reason you're doing this is to not finance your vacation but to build your credit worthiness (and credit score) as fast as you can.

It doesn't take much effort either. Let's say you open one of these accounts. Maybe they give you $500. Credit limit. Maybe they require you to secure it in half. Just do it.

Then, start using it – sparingly. If you need to buy a few things at the store, use the card. Then, immediately pay the balance on the card. Do this a few times per month, and you will see your score grow. If you are buying something a bit bigger than you cannot pay all at once, that is also good. This is how the credit card companies make money. Just be sure to pay it down over the next few months.

A good rule of thumb is to have the money in the bank when you buy something. I know that is not always possible, but doing this will help you.

If you're paying rent every month, see if your landlord will report your payments to the big three credit bureaus. If not, there are third-party services out there that you can find that will do this for a small fee. Basically, you sign up, pay the vig, and they verify and report your rent payment on your credit report. This is important because this is usually your biggest monthly expense. A good regular report of monthly payments will help your score big time.

I mean, if your mortgage is reportable, your rent should be too. It's the biggest expense!

Another idea is to apply for one of those subprime loans offered through Websites. They are very expensive but will build your credit fast.

Basically, you need a steady stream of verifiable income. They charge huge money in interest rates which compensates for their risk. Credit scores are secondary to the ability to pay.

Let's say you apply for a $3000 personal loan from one of these sites. In three days, they wire you the money to your account. Put that money in your savings and keep it there. Make the first one or two payments on the loan, they pay it off with the savings. You will have paid the loan, improved your credit rating and they will be begging you to take out another lower interest loan!

You need discipline. Having the money in your account could be a temptation to spend. Don't! Even if you have to give the money to your trusted friend of the mother. Whatever it takes, don't spend it. Use it to pay the loan in 2 months.

If you're successful you can repeat this a few times. Don't go overboard, just a few times within a year to a year and a half. This will really boost your score.

When you are doing the right thing, you will see more ads soliciting you for more credit cards. I would encourage you to get the best deal and not go overboard. Having two cards is usually enough.

If you're having issues getting a card, even a secured card, try a store credit card. I hate store credit cards and don't see the need for them, but they are generally easier to get. Apply for a store credit card while you make a purchase, and you will almost certainly get the card. Sure, the limit will be super low, but so what. It's a start.

Credit utilizations are an important measure of your credit worthiness. Ok, so having a credit card has its perks but comes with responsibilities. So let's say you started from scratch and are rebuilding. You want to make sure that your overall balances don't exceed 30-40% of the total credit limit. That's called utilization. If you have your cards maxed out, that's a sign. If you have no balances and do you the cards, that's also bad. You need to keep a happy medium. Use the cards, pay the bills and do this responsibly and your credit opportunities will improve. No longer will you be offered 25% interest rates. You will be in the low risk markets that are favorable to conservative creditors. This makes buying a home, renting an apartment and getting a decent job much easier.

Use Websites like bankrate.com to get some ideas on first time or bad credit lenders and credit card companies. They can also get your credit score for you easily too. It's something you should be on top of since it impacts your life in so many ways.

IN MASSACHUSETTS

Massachusetts is a land steeped in history. I love history and love being surrounded by it, especially where I can laugh and say "they really did that?"

For all of you in the rest of the world, we here still have laws on the books that regulate the grazing of cattle on the Boston Common and regulations about drinking coffee on Sunday, especially before noon. These "old blue laws" were developed and passed before, during and after the revolution. So if you're planning on grazing your cattle, good luck getting them onto the common from the subway and across Tremont St.

Not quite as old but definitely archaic was our legislation on certain crimes, reporting, and mandatory sentences.

But, on April 13th, 2018, Governor Baker signed into law the first comprehensive legislation criminal justice reform bill the Commonwealth has seen in decades! This legislation includes many positive reforms:

- Reforms CORI Law so that people in long-term recovery can overcome the burden of a criminal record.

- Reduces CORI sealing times to 7 years for felonies and 3 years for misdemeanors instead of the current 10 years for felonies and 5 years for misdemeanors.

The new law makes resisting arrest convictions sealable.

Allows people with sealed records to say "I have no record" on housing and professional licensure applications.

It also raises the minimum dollar amount for charging felony theft from $250 (third lowest in the nation) to $1,200 so that minor theft does not result in a long felony record. It reduces fines and fees for probation/parole that people in early recovery sometimes struggle to pay. It mandates District Attorneys create diversion programs for people with addictions and makes more people eligible for diversion so that people with addiction get a chance at treatment rather than jail.

It eliminates some mandatory minimum sentences for nonviolent offenses to give sentencing discretion back to judges and allow for diversion to treatment rather than jail for people struggling with addictions.

As someone who understands recovery, this is great news. Somehow, they seemed to understand that many low-level drug dealers struggle with addiction themselves and need treatment rather than long prison sentences.

There is hope.

Made in the USA
Middletown, DE
14 December 2018